The Usborne Kings and Queens Sticker Book

Sarah Courtauld & Kate Davies
Illustrated by Adam Larkum

Designed by Laura Wood

Edited by Jane Chisholm

Contents

Early English kings

Around 1500 years ago, England was made up of seven small kingdoms, each with their own king. During the 9th century, the people living in these kingdoms began to call themselves 'the English', and became united under one king.

Alfred ruled Wessex, an area of southern England. He spent most of his reign fighting off Viking raiders from Scandinavia. Eventually he saved his kingdom from the Vikings, and became known as 'King of the English.' His achievements in peace and war earned him the title 'the Great.'

Alfred the Great
871–899

Cnut was a Viking invader who conquered a large area of England and managed to become King.

A story says Cnut's nobles thought he had godlike powers. Cnut took his throne to the beach and ordered the tide not to come in. Cnut got wet, and his nobles realized he was just human.

Edward was known as 'the Confessor,' because he was very religious. England was at peace during his reign. But he had no children, so when he died in 1066, three men fought for the crown. One of them, William, Duke of Normandy (in France), invaded and made himself King.

This picture shows Edward the Confessor seeing a vision of Christ. Edward is the man wearing the crown. He was made a saint after he died.

William, known as 'the Conqueror,' introduced French laws and made French the language of government. English nobles hated him because he kicked them out of their homes and jobs so his friends could have them.

William wanted to raise taxes, so he ordered a huge survey of how much land and money everyone had. This was called the Domesday Book.

This picture of William the Conqueror is from the Bayeux Tapestry, a famous embroidery made to commemorate the Norman invasion.

William II was known as William 'Rufus,' which means 'red' – probably because he had red hair and a red face. He had a fiery temper, too.

William was killed by an arrow while he was hunting. Some people think his brother, Henry, had him killed, so he could be King.

Henry I only had two children with his wife – a son named William, and a daughter named Matilda – but 26 with his many girlfriends.

Henry I
1100–1135

But Henry's son and heir, William, died in 1120 when a boat he was sailing in, the *White Ship*, sank in the English Channel. Henry was heartbroken.

Henry died suddenly in 1135, apparently after eating too many lampreys – tiny eels with sucker-like mouths and lots of sharp teeth.

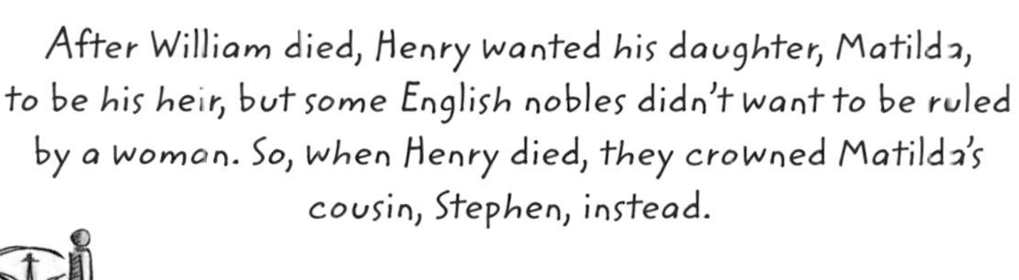

After William died, Henry wanted his daughter, Matilda, to be his heir, but some English nobles didn't want to be ruled by a woman. So, when Henry died, they crowned Matilda's cousin, Stephen, instead.

Stephen was kind and good-tempered. But he was lazy, and he struggled to control his subjects – probably because he wasn't terrifying enough.

Stephen
1135–1154

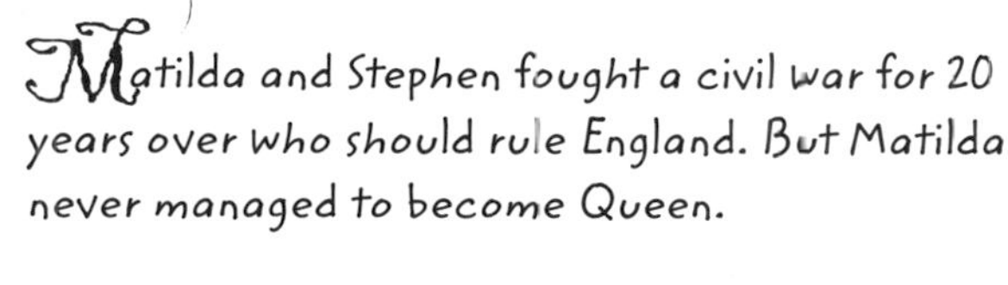

Matilda and Stephen fought a civil war for 20 years over who should rule England. But Matilda never managed to become Queen.

In 1141, Matilda was held prisoner in a castle in Oxford – but she escaped. The ground was covered with snow, so Matilda dressed in white, and no one noticed her run away.

Matilda won in the end. Stephen didn't leave any heirs, so after he died, Matilda's son Henry became King.

Early Scottish kings

Many early Scottish kings spent their reigns fighting the English, who wanted to rule Scotland. It wasn't until Robert the Bruce's reign that England recognized Scotland as an independent nation. Here are some of the most important early kings of Scotland.

Macbeth came to the throne of Scotland after he killed his cousin, King Duncan, in a battle. Macbeth was a strong ruler and reigned peacefully for 17 years. But, in 1057, Duncan's son Malcolm killed Macbeth, and became Malcolm III.

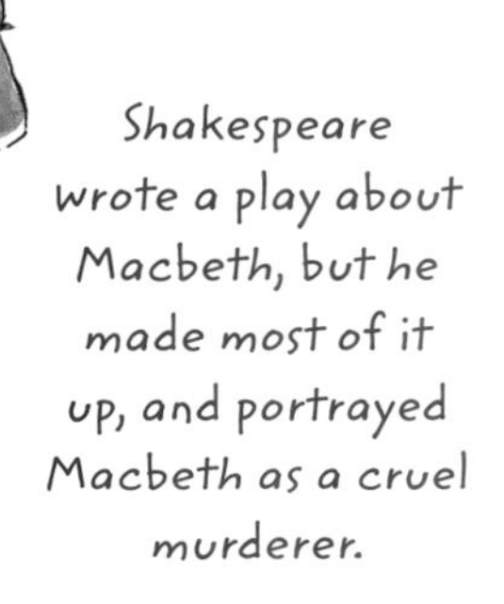

Shakespeare wrote a play about Macbeth, but he made most of it up, and portrayed Macbeth as a cruel murderer.

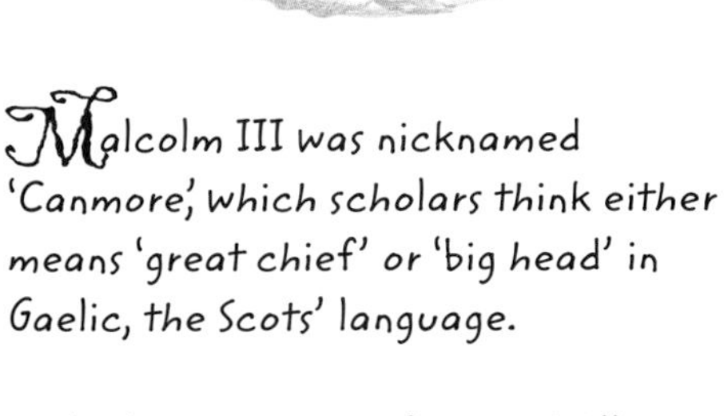

Malcolm III was nicknamed 'Canmore', which scholars think either means 'great chief' or 'big head' in Gaelic, the Scots' language.

Malcolm spent years fighting William the Conqueror. In 1072 they made a peace deal, and William made Malcolm hand over his son, Duncan, to guarantee he'd obey him. But war broke out again 10 years later, and Malcolm was killed.

Malcolm was devoted to his wife Margaret, even though they spoke different languages: Malcolm spoke Gaelic, and Margaret spoke English. She was very religious, helped poor people, and was later declared a saint.

David I spent most of his childhood in England, at the court of Henry I. He married Matilda, the daughter of a powerful English noble. When David became King, he introduced the first coins to Scotland.

This picture shows David I with his grandson, who succeeded him as Malcolm IV.

Alexander III is remembered as one of Scotland's greatest rulers, because Scotland was peaceful and prosperous during his reign.

But, one rainy night, he fell off his horse and broke his neck. His granddaughter Margaret was meant to succeed him, but she died on her way to Scotland.

Alexander III
1249–1286

Several men wanted to be King after Alexander, so the Scottish nobles asked King Edward I of England to decide who should rule Scotland next. He chose John Balliol, but he wouldn't let him have any real power.

In 1296, Edward invaded Scotland and locked John Balliol in the Tower of London. After that, Scotland didn't have a king again until 1306.

John Balliol
1292–1296

In 1297, the Scots rebelled against the English. Led by a nobleman named William Wallace, they beat Edward's army at the Battle of Stirling Bridge, but eventually Wallace was caught and executed. He became a great Scottish hero.

Robert I, also known by his family name Robert the Bruce, rebelled against England along with William Wallace. He fought hard to become King of Scotland, and in 1306 he was finally crowned. But he spent years fighting the English. Eventually, he defeated them at the Battle of Bannockburn, and got them to agree that Scotland was an independent nation.

Robert I
1306–1329

According to one legend, during his struggle for Scottish independence Robert the Bruce was encouraged to keep fighting the English by watching a spider trying to spin a web. The spider kept falling down, but it kept on trying and trying, and at last it succeeded.

The Plantagenets

When Stephen, last of the Norman kings, died without an heir, Matilda's son, Henry of Anjou, became Henry II. He was the first of the Plantagenet kings. Most of them were great warriors, but lots were very bad tempered, too.

Henry II was a good ruler, but he argued for over ten years with his friend, Thomas Becket, the Archbishop of Canterbury. One day Henry shouted, "Will no one rid me of this troublesome priest?" Four knights overheard him, and murdered Becket.

Henry was horrified. He didn't really want Becket killed. To show how sorry he was, he walked barefoot to Canterbury Cathedral, wearing sack cloth.

The Plantagenets got their name from Henry's father, Geoffrey of Anjou. He always wore sprigs of broom flowers (*planta genista* in Latin) in his hat.

Henry II
1154–1189

Richard I was known as 'the Lionheart,' because of his bravery in battle. He spent more time fighting wars overseas than ruling the country – in fact, he was only in England for 6 months of his 10-year reign.

Richard I
1189–1199

This illustration from a medieval manuscript shows Richard fighting Saladin, a Muslim ruler, during religious wars known as the Crusades. Saladin is painted with a blue face, to make him look evil.

John refused to listen to his powerful advisers, and he made them pay lots of taxes. So they turned against him and made him sign a document known as *Magna Carta*. It said that even kings had consult their advisers, and not just do whatever they wanted.

John
1199–1216

King John appears as Robin Hood's enemy in the Robin Hood legends.

Henry III spent much of his reign fighting against *Magna Carta.* In 1256, the nobles demanded he call a Great Council of lords and bishops to help him decide important things. This was the first Parliament. Eventually the nobles overthrew him, but with the help of his son Edward, he raised an army and became King again.

Henry III kept all sorts of animals, including a polar bear, in a zoo at the Tower of London.

Henry III
1216–1272

Edward I was nicknamed 'long-shanks' because his legs were so long. He spent years trying to conquer the Scots, and fought them so often that his tombstone reads: "Here lies Edward, the Hammer of the Scots."

This picture shows Edward I making his son (the future Edward II) the Prince of Wales.

Edward I
1272–1307

Edward II was close friends with two noblemen. He showered them with gifts and gave them lots of power. This annoyed the other nobles, who had one of them murdered. It annoyed the Queen even more. She raised an army to overthrow her husband, and put their 14-year-old son on the throne, as King Edward III. Eventually, Edward II was murdered with a red-hot poker.

Edward II
1307–1327

Edward III
1327–1377

Edward III was a much more successful king than his father. He held lavish festivals and jousting tournaments, and founded the Order of the Garter, an order of knighthood that still exists today. Edward III's beloved son Edward, the 'Black Prince' died in battle, so when he died his grandson Richard became Richard II.

Richard II
1377–1399

Richard II had a turbulent reign. When he was 17, the peasants rebelled against him. The revolt was crushed, but eventually the nobles rose up against him, too, because Richard didn't think he should have to take advice from them. He was overthrown, and his cousin Henry became King.

Richard was imprisoned in Pontefract Castle, where he died. Some said he starved himself, but others said he was murdered.

Richard spent lots of money on fancy clothes, such as shoes which tied at the knee. He also introduced forks and handkerchiefs to England.

The white rose of York

The Wars of the Roses

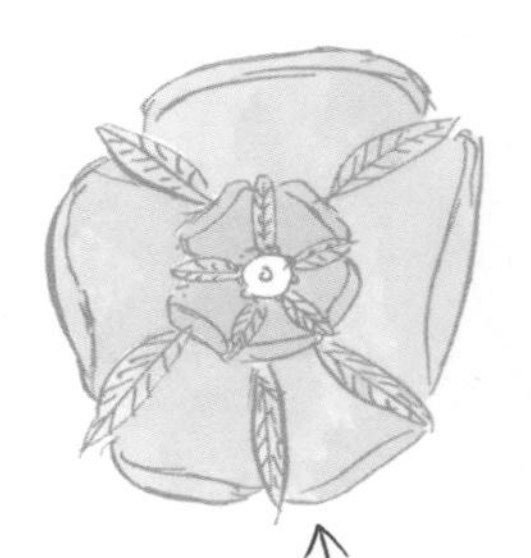

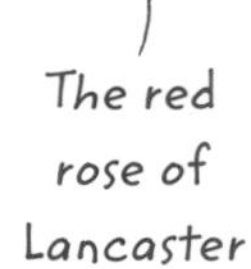

The red rose of Lancaster

The House of Lancaster and the House of York were both branches of the Plantagenet family, but they didn't get on. In 1461, a civil war broke out between the two houses. It lasted for 30 years.

Henry, Duke of Lancaster, seized the crown from his unpopular cousin Richard II, making himself Henry IV. Most people were glad Richard was gone, but Henry still had to fight to keep his crown. He found being King exhausting, and eventually he became ill and died.

Henry IV
1399–1413

Henry V is remembered as one of England's greatest monarchs, even though he was King for just nine years.

Henry was a brilliant soldier, who won a major victory against the French at the Battle of Agincourt in 1415. He wanted to be King of France as well as England. He almost managed it, too – but he died before he could be crowned.

Henry V
1413–1422

Henry VI wasn't a natural leader. He was gentle and religious and hated violence. He also suffered from bouts of madness. Eventually his cousin Richard, Duke of York challenged him for the crown. It was war.

The conflict between the Yorkists and the Lancastrians became known as the Wars of the Roses, because each side had a rose as their family emblem.

Henry VI
1422–1461, 1470–1471

The Yorkists imprisoned Henry VI in the Tower of London – but their leader, Richard, Duke of York, was killed in battle. So Richard's son, Edward, was crowned, and became Edward IV.

Edward IV was King twice. He was driven from the throne in 1470, after he angered his nobles by ignoring their advice and marrying a woman from a non-noble family. Edward fled to France, and Henry VI was given a second chance at ruling the country. But Edward fought back. A year later he became King again, and Henry died mysteriously in the Tower of London.

This picture shows Edward escaping to France.

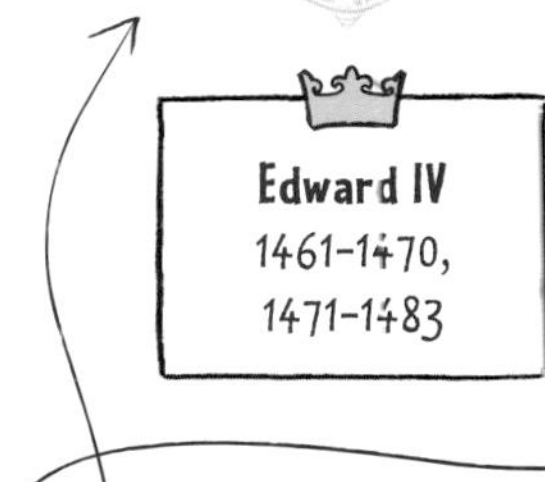

Edward IV
1461-1470,
1471-1483

Edward is the man in the red coat.

Edward V was only 13 when he became King, but he was never crowned – his uncle Richard imprisoned him in the Tower of London with his little brother, and had himself crowned instead.

The brothers became known as the 'Princes in the Tower'. At first, people used to see them playing in the Tower gardens, but soon they disappeared. Most people thought Richard had murdered them. In 1674, two skeletons were found in the Tower. They might be the remains of the two princes.

Edward V
1483

Richard III was handsome, brave and a skilled ruler. But he was thought to have murdered his two young nephews, so he wasn't very popular.

Richard was the last King of England to die in battle. He was defeated by his cousin, Henry Tudor, at the Battle of Bosworth in 1485. This marked the end of the Wars of the Roses – and of the Plantagenet dynasty.

Richard III
1483-1485

When Richard died, the new King, Henry VII, spread lots of nasty stories about him. About 100 years later, Shakespeare wrote a play about Richard III, portraying him as an evil man with a hunched back.

The Tudors

Henry Tudor seized the throne, ending the Wars of the Roses and becoming the first Tudor monarch – Henry VII. His son, Henry VIII, became one of the most famous monarchs in history. He married six times and made himself head of the Church in England.

Henry VII didn't have a very good claim to the throne, so lots of people tried to take it from him. One was a boy called Lambert Simnel, who pretended he was the nephew of Edward IV. When he was found out, Henry made him work in the royal kitchens as a punishment.

Henry VII
1485–1509

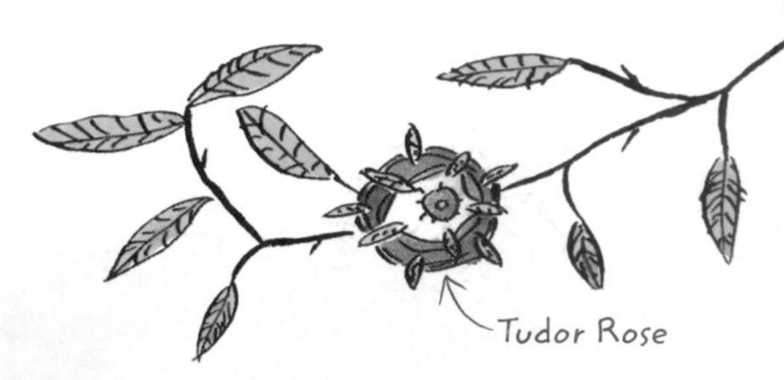

Tudor Rose

Henry VII was a member of the Lancaster family, but when he married Elizabeth of York, he united the two warring sides. He created a new emblem, the Tudor Rose, made up of the red rose of Lancaster and the white rose of York.

Henry VIII
1509–1547

Henry VIII was handsome, charming and clever as a young man. But as he grew older, he became more and more bad tempered, and executed people if they disagreed with him.

Henry loved playing indoor tennis... but most people didn't dare beat him.

Henry was desperate to have a son, but his first wife, Catherine of Aragon, only gave birth to a daughter – Mary. So Henry decided to divorce her.

But, the trouble was, the Catholic Church wouldn't allow him to divorce. So Henry cut himself off from the Pope, the head of the Catholic Church in Rome. He made himself head of the Church in England, and granted himself a divorce.

Catherine of Aragon
Queen 1509–1533
Divorced

After Henry VIII divorced Catherine of Aragon, he married five more times.

First he fell in love with a courtier named Anne Boleyn. She gave birth to a daughter, Elizabeth. But, like Catherine of Aragon, she didn't have a son. Henry grew tired of her, and had her executed.

Anne Boleyn
Queen 1533-1536
Beheaded

Some people who resented Anne spread gossip that she had six fingers on each hand and was a witch.

Just 11 days after Anne's execution, Henry married Jane Seymour. She gave birth to a son, Edward, but she died soon after.

Jane Seymour
Queen 1536-1537
Died

Next, Henry married Anne of Cleves. Henry hadn't met Anne before he agreed to marry her – he'd only seen this flattering portrait of her. When he met her, he thought she was ugly, and divorced her soon after.

Anne of Cleves
Queen 1540
Divorced

Henry married 19-year-old Catherine Howard the same year he divorced Anne of Cleves. Catherine was 30 years younger than Henry. She didn't like her new husband and had a romance with another man. When Henry found out, he had her executed.

Catherine Howard
Queen 1540-1542
Beheaded

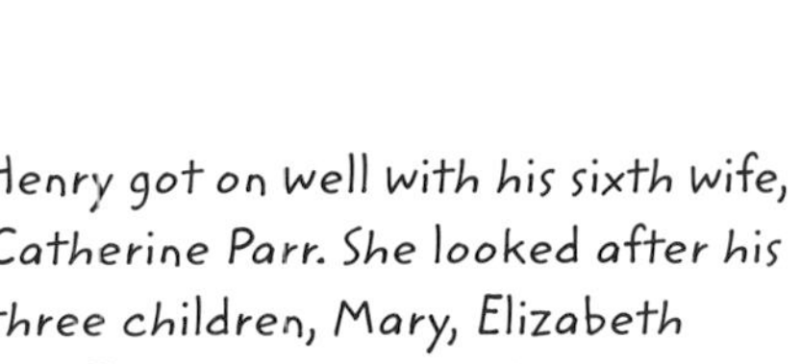

Henry got on well with his sixth wife, Catherine Parr. She looked after his three children, Mary, Elizabeth and Edward, and stayed with Henry until he died.

Catherine Parr
Queen 1543-1547
Survived

By the time he died, Henry was grumpy, sick, and so fat that he couldn't walk.

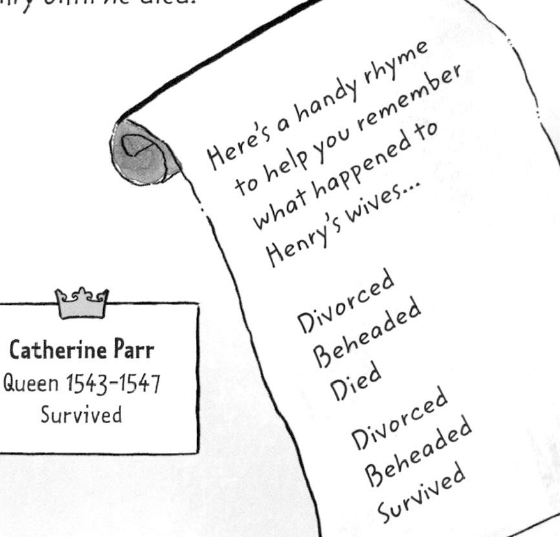

More Tudors

Henry VIII had been desperate for a son to secure the Tudor dynasty, but his son, Edward VI, died young. Edward was succeeded by his sisters, Mary and Elizabeth, who showed that women could rule just as well as men. In fact, Elizabeth proved to be one of the greatest monarchs in British history.

Edward VI came to the throne when he was nine years old. Serious and clever, he and his advisers reformed the Church and made England a truly Protestant country. People had high hopes for him, but Edward died when he was just 15.

Edward VI
1547-1553

Rich nobles used to slip the young King Edward extra pocket money when his strict guardians weren't looking.

Edward named Lady Jane Grey as his heir, because he didn't want his Catholic sister Mary to rule the country. But, before Jane could be crowned, Mary raised an army and seized the throne. Jane was executed, after ruling for just nine days.

This is a 19th century painting of Lady Jane Grey's execution. The artist gave her white clothes to make her look like an innocent victim.

Lady Jane Grey
July 1553

Mary was fiery-tempered, like her father, Henry VIII, and she made herself unpopular by trying to make England a Catholic country again. She was nicknamed 'Bloody Mary' because she had over 300 people burned to death for refusing to become Catholic.

Mary I
1553-1558

When Mary was a young woman, her father divorced her mother, and she was sent away from court. She was even made to act as a servant to her half-sister, Elizabeth.

When Elizabeth I first came to the throne, everyone wondered who she would marry. But Elizabeth didn't want a husband – she didn't want to share her power. She stayed single all her life, claiming she was married to her country.

Elizabeth sometimes toured the country, expecting noblemen to give her luxurious places to stay. Nobles spent huge amounts of money trying to please her. Some even converted their houses into the shape of an E.

Elizabeth I
1558–1603

The portrait on the right was made to celebrate the defeat of the Spanish Armada – a fleet of ships sent by the Spanish King to conquer England in 1588. Elizabeth gave a famous speech to her troops, saying, "I may have the body of a weak and feeble woman, but I have the heart and stomach of a king."

This part of the painting shows the Spanish ships approaching England...

...and this part shows the ships being wrecked in a storm.

Elizabeth wore lots of white make-up to make herself look fashionably pale. But the make-up was made of poisonous lead, and it made her ill.

Although Elizabeth never married, there were many men whose company she enjoyed. They included Sir Walter Raleigh, an explorer who introduced two American plants, tobacco and potatoes, to England.

Elizabeth was also very fond of Sir Francis Drake, the first Englishman to sail all the way around the world.

Francis Drake's ship, the *Golden Hinde*.

The Scottish Stewarts

In 1371, Robert II, grandson of Robert the Bruce, became the first Stewart King of Scotland. The Stewart kings faced lots of challenges: rebels, pirates, kidnappers and, worst of all, the English.

Robert II was 54 when he became King. He was nicknamed 'Auld Blearie,' which means 'old watery-eyed.' Soon, he was too decrepit to be a very good ruler.

Robert II
1371-1390

THAN ROBERT STEVART YE SECVND
IN YAT RING THAT DID SVCCEID OF
SCOTLAND TO BE KING MARIIT AGNES
DRVMOND ANE LADY BRICHT DOCHTER
TO SCHIR JOHN DRVMOND OF STOBHAL
KNYCHT

This illustration shows Robert III with his wife, Annabella.

Robert III had a difficult reign. A kick from a horse left him barely able to walk, and his own brother kidnapped his son and starved him to death.

The thistle is a symbol of the Stewart family.

Robert sent his second son, James, to France to keep him safe, but the boy was captured by pirates and then held prisoner by the King of England.

Robert III
1390-1406

Robert III died soon after, asking this to be written on his gravestone: "Here lies the worst of kings and the most miserable of men."

James I was 12 when he was imprisoned by the King of England, and 30 by the time he got out. He became a strong ruler, but he still had enemies. In 1437, he was murdered by a group of nobles while he was staying in a monastery.

James I
1406-1437

James fell in love with his future wife, Joan Beaufort, when he saw her from his prison window. She inspired him to write a love poem that was 1,387 lines long.

James II
1437-1460

James II had a red birthmark on one side of his face, which led to the nickname, 'fiery face.' He was ruthless at putting down uprisings, and personally stabbed to death his most rebellious subject, the Earl of Douglas.

James III
1460–1488

James III made himself unpopular in Scotland by trying to make peace with the English. The Scottish nobles wanted war – so they started an uprising against him. James died in 1488, after he was injured in a battle against the nobles.

James IV was very well-educated. He spoke six languages, and welcomed lots of poets to his court. During his reign, the first printing press in Scotland was built.

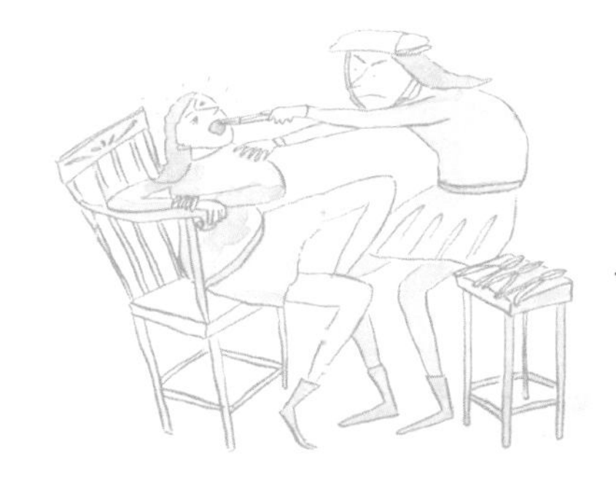

James IV was also interested in science, and tried his hand at medicine and dentistry.

According to legend, James V got the nickname 'King of the Commons', because he liked wandering around Scotland disguised as a farmer so he could meet ordinary people.

This gold crown was made for James V. He first wore it at the coronation of his second Queen, Mary of Guise.

James V died in battle against the English King Henry VIII and was succeeded by his one-month-old daughter, Mary.

Mary Stewart changed her name to the French spelling, 'Stuart', when she was married to the King of France. After he died, she married a man named Darnley, who died in suspicious circumstances.

When she married the man thought to have killed Darnley, there was an uprising against her and she fled to England.

But in England, her cousin, Elizabeth I, suspected that she was plotting against her. She locked Mary up for 19 years and eventually had her executed.

Mary had a pet dog that went everywhere with her. It even went to her execution, hiding under her skirts.

The Stuarts

When Queen Elizabeth died childless, Mary Stuart's son, James VI of Scotland, became James I, the first Stuart king of England. Not everyone liked him, but they disliked his son Charles even more. Eventually Charles got his head chopped off.

James VI and I
King of Scots 1567–1625
King of England and Ireland 1603–1625

James was only 13 months old when he became King of Scotland, in 1567. In 1603 he was crowned King of England, too.

James was scared of assassins, and wore a padded suit to protect him from being stabbed.

James was terrified that people wanted to kill him... and he was right. One group of Catholic terrorists planned to blow up Parliament with the King inside it.

Luckily for James, the plotters were found out and executed. Every year, people in England celebrate the Fifth of November, the night when the gunpowder plot was discovered, with bonfires and fireworks.

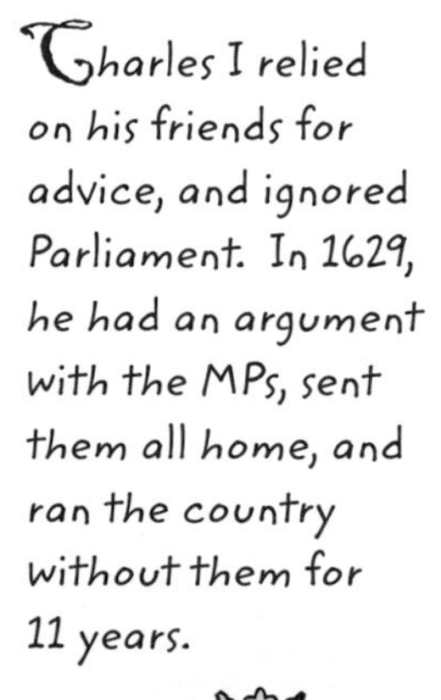

Charles I relied on his friends for advice, and ignored Parliament. In 1629, he had an argument with the MPs, sent them all home, and ran the country without them for 11 years.

Charles I
1625–1649

Charles I was married to a French princess called Henrietta Maria. As a Catholic, she was unpopular with the British public.

Henrietta Maria and Charles were very fond of their court jester, a dwarf named Jeffrey. He once jumped out of a pie, dressed as a knight.

As time went on, the situation between Charles and Parliament grew worse and worse, until in 1642 civil war broke out.

On one side were Charles and his supporters, the Royalists; on the other side were the Parliamentarians, led by an MP named Oliver Cromwell.

The Royalists called Parliamentarian soldiers 'Roundheads', because they wore round metal helmets.

The Royalist soldiers became known as 'Cavaliers'. The Parliamentarians thought they were vain and lazy.

One of the leading Cavaliers was Prince Rupert of the Rhine, Charles's nephew.

After seven years, Cromwell's army defeated the Royalists. Charles was put on trial for treason, and sentenced to death. He was executed on January 30, 1649.

After Charles's death, his son, also called Charles, fought against Cromwell. But in 1651 he was defeated and went on the run. He was nearly caught by some of Cromwell's soldiers, but he hid in an oak tree until they'd gone. Soon afterwards, he managed to flee to France.

After the execution of Charles I, the country was ruled by Oliver Cromwell, who led a government known as the Commonwealth.

Cromwell was very religious, and he believed that people should lead simple, hard-working lives. He banned drinking, gambling, and dancing, as well as Christmas and Easter celebrations.

Oliver Cromwell
1649–1660

Restoring the Stuarts

When Oliver Cromwell died, his son Richard was put in charge. But he didn't want the job, and no one wanted him as their leader. The Scots had already crowned Charles II, and it wasn't long before the people of England wanted a king back on the throne, too.

Known as the 'Merry Monarch,' Charles II could not have been less like Oliver Cromwell. He re-opened the playhouses and introduced champagne to Britain.

Charles II
1660–1685

Charles loved racing yachts, and kept a boat called the *Royal Escape* moored on the Thames. Charles had used it to flee the country during the civil war.

Soon after Charles became King, he faced two terrible events. First, in 1665, a deadly plague spread through London. Then, less than a year later, a huge fire swept through the city.

This is a portrait of Samuel Pepys, who witnessed the fire and wrote about it in his diary.

He buried his wine, cheese and papers in his garden, to keep them safe from the flames.

When Charles died, his younger brother James became King. James was a Catholic, and he kept giving powerful jobs to his Catholic friends, which made many Protestant politicians angry.

So a group of politicians wrote to the Dutch Protestant Prince, William of Orange, who was married to James's daughter. They asked him to invade and take over.

When William of Orange invaded, James fled to France without a fight.

James II
1685–1688

William and his wife Mary were the only monarchs to rule together, as equals. When they first met, Mary didn't think much of William, who was much older and shorter than her, and had black teeth. She wept throughout their wedding.

But once they were married, she and William became a devoted couple.

William and Mary
1689–1702

When Mary died, in 1694, William said he was "the miserablest creature on earth".

William ruled alone for eight years. Then, while he was out riding one day, his horse tripped over a molehill. He fell off, broke his collarbone, and died a few days later.

After William's death, Mary's sister Anne became Queen. She suffered badly from gout, and had to be carried to her coronation in a large chair.

Anne
1702–1714

In 1707, an act of parliament, called the Act of Union, joined the kingdoms of England and Scotland. They became the United Kingdom of Great Britain.

Queen Anne had at least 17 pregnancies, but none of her children survived. When she died, Stuart rule came to an end.

The Hanoverians

After Queen Anne died childless, her cousin George, from Hanover in Germany, took the throne as George I. Over the following hundred years, there were four kings called George – so this is often known as the Georgian age.

When George I became King, he was 54 years old, and hardly spoke any English.

More than fifty Catholics were more closely related to Anne, but George was chosen because he was a Protestant.

George I
1714–1727

George I brought a famous composer, George Frideric Handel, with him to London.

Handel wrote lots of famous pieces for him, including the *Water Music*, which he composed for a concert on the River Thames.

During George's reign, Britain got its first ever Prime Minister, Robert Walpole. He lived at 10 Downing Street, where British prime ministers still live today. This picture shows Walpole giving a speech to his ministers.

Some people thought that James Stuart, Queen Anne's half-brother, was the rightful heir to the throne.

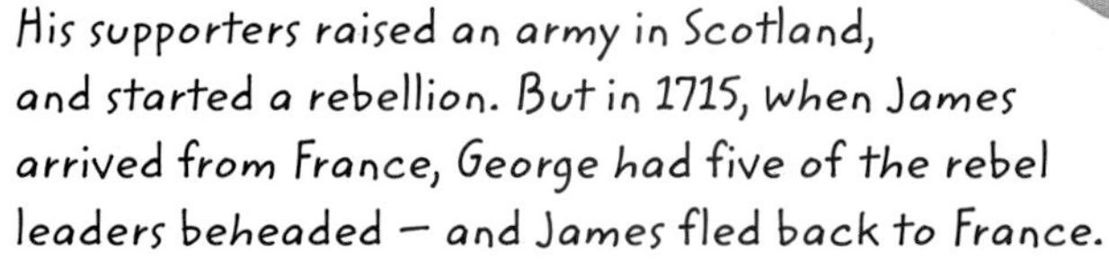

His supporters raised an army in Scotland, and started a rebellion. But in 1715, when James arrived from France, George had five of the rebel leaders beheaded – and James fled back to France.

George II never got on with his father, George I.

When he was a little boy, his father divorced his mother for having an affair, and locked her up in a castle for the rest of her life.

When he was a teenager, it is said that George tried to swim across the castle moat to see her – but was hauled out before he made it.

George II never forgave his father, and they argued constantly.

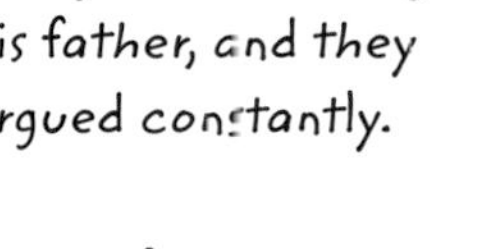

George II
1727–1760

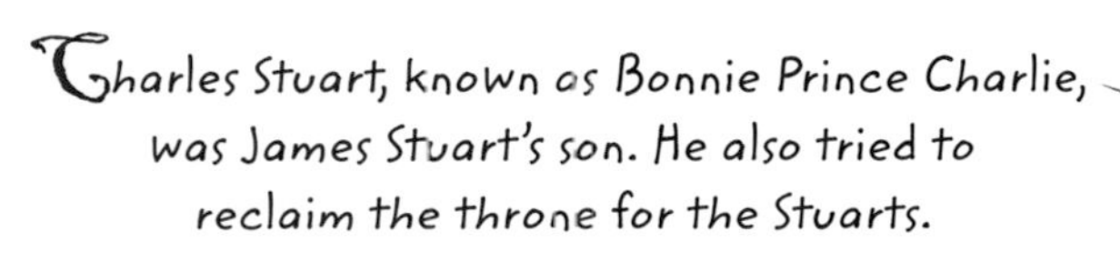

Charles Stuart, known as Bonnie Prince Charlie, was James Stuart's son. He also tried to reclaim the throne for the Stuarts.

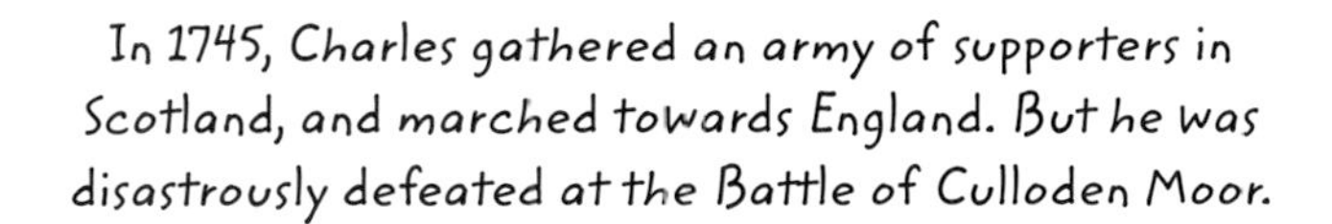

In 1745, Charles gathered an army of supporters in Scotland, and marched towards England. But he was disastrously defeated at the Battle of Culloden Moor.

After his defeat, Charlie went on the run – and the government promised £30,000 to anyone who could capture him.

A woman named Flora MacDonald helped Charlie flee to the Isle of Skye, disguised as her maid. From there, he escaped on a boat to France.

More Hanoverians

George III was a very popular king, but he developed an illness that made people think he was insane, so his son, George IV, ruled in his place. After George IV's death, his brother William IV became the oldest person ever to take the throne.

George III
1760–1820

George III's down-to-earth manner made him a much loved King.

One of George III's hobbies was farming – he was known as 'Farmer George'.

George III was devoted to his wife, Queen Charlotte. They called each other Mr. and Mrs. King.

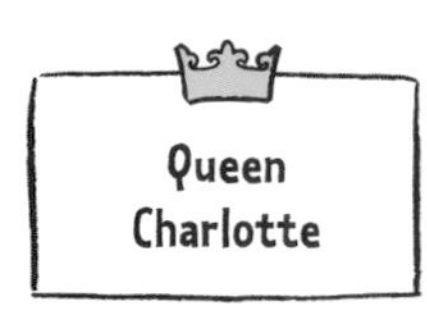

Queen Charlotte

When George was ill, he suffered from some strange symptoms. It was said that he once had a conversation with a tree, thinking that it was the King of Prussia.

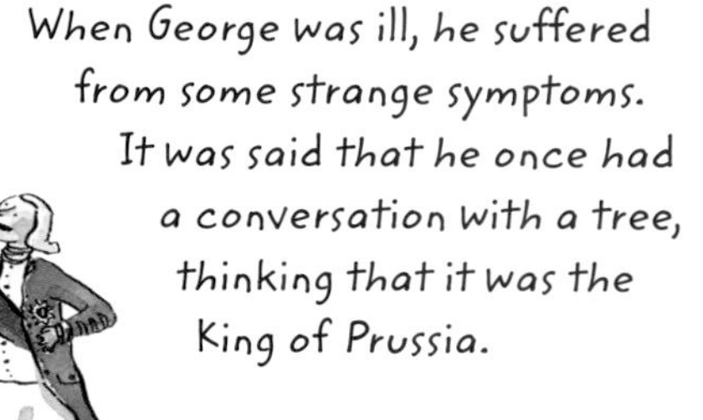

When his doctors failed to cure him, his son George became Prince Regent, ruling on behalf of his father.

George IV
1820–1830

George IV was cultured and intelligent, but also very extravagant. He built an enormous, Oriental-style palace, called the Royal Pavillion, beside the sea in Brighton.

When George IV became overweight, artists mocked him in their cartoons.

Queen Caroline

George enjoyed the novels of a witty writer named Jane Austen. She dedicated one of her novels, *Emma*, to him – but only after his librarian asked her to.

George IV's wife, Caroline of Brunswick, was not fond of washing and liked eating onions. After just a year of marriage, George refused to see his wife.

When Caroline tried to go to her husband's coronation, the door was slammed in her face. She banged on the door, shouting: "I am the Queen of England!" – but no one let her in.

William IV was 64 years old when he became King. He had spent most of his life in the Royal Navy, so he was nicknamed 'The Sailor King.'

During William's reign, new laws abolished slavery and made the voting system fairer.

William IV had a beautiful mistress, an actress known as Dorothea Jordan. They had ten children together but, as the couple never married, their children weren't heirs to the throne. When William died, his niece Princess Victoria became Queen.

William IV
1830–1837

Queen Victoria

and the House of Saxe-Coburg-Gotha

Queen Victoria ruled Britain for longer than any other monarch. While she was Queen, Britain had the largest empire in history, and by the end of her reign, new inventions had changed the country forever.

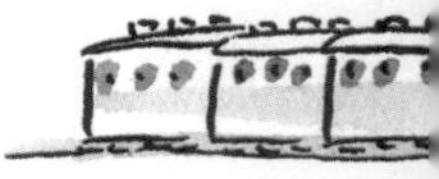

Victoria
1837–1901

Victoria became Queen at the age of 18. She took her royal duties very seriously, and studied history as a child so she could learn from previous monarchs. She hoped to do better than Elizabeth I, who she thought was a great Queen but a bad woman.

In 1840, Victoria married her German cousin, Albert of Saxe-Coburg-Gotha. Victoria and Albert were devoted to each other. Albert supported Victoria in her royal duties, and she gave him the title Prince Consort, to show how important he was to her and the country.

Victoria and Albert had nine children. This picture shows them with their family at Christmas. Prince Albert brought to Britain the German traditions of decorating Christmas trees and sending Christmas cards.

The world's first postage stamp, the 'Penny Black,' was introduced in 1840. It had Victoria's head on it.

During Victoria's reign all kinds of new machines were invented, the first railways were built, and lots of people moved to cities to work in new factories. This was known as the Industrial Revolution.

Prince Albert helped organize the Great Exhibition of 1851, to show off inventions from Britain and around the world. It was held in the Crystal Palace in Hyde Park – the largest glass building ever built.

During Victoria's reign, the British Empire stretched all around the world, and Victoria was made Empress of India. She never went to India, but she learned to speak Hindi and Urdu, and had an Indian adviser to help her.

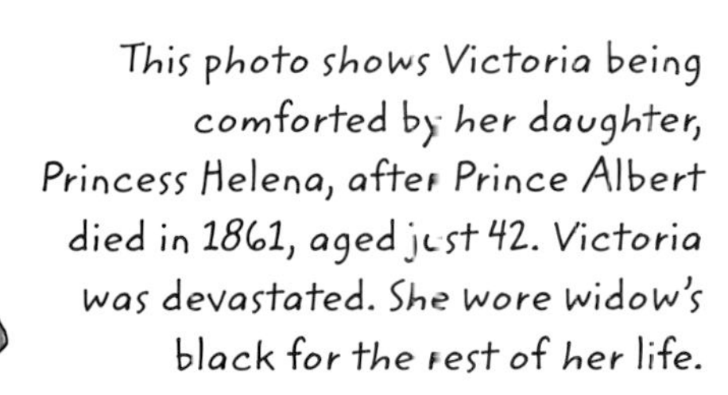

This photo shows Victoria being comforted by her daughter, Princess Helena, after Prince Albert died in 1861, aged just 42. Victoria was devastated. She wore widow's black for the rest of her life.

Victoria lived for another 40 years. When she died in 1901, thousands of people lined the streets to watch her funeral procession.

Edward VII was Victoria and Albert's eldest son. He was heir to the throne for 60 years – longer than any other British monarch. He drank a lot, ate a lot, and loved expensive parties, hunting and gambling.

Edward was a charming, popular and generous king. But he died after just nine years on the throne.

Edward was devoted to his pet dog, Caesar. He took him everywhere and gave him a collar with "I belong to the king" inscribed on it. When Edward died, Caesar walked in the funeral procession.

The Windsors

When Victoria married Albert, the royal family took his name – Saxe-Coburg-Gotha. But when the First World War broke out, George V thought the name sounded too German, so he renamed his family Windsor, after Windsor Castle.

George V trained to be an officer in the navy before he became King. He loved sailing, and even had traditional sailor tattoos on his arms.

This photo shows George V giving a speech over the radio. He decided to broadcast a message to his people every Christmas. The tradition of the royal Christmas message continues today.

Edward VIII was King for less than a year. He fell in love with an American divorcee named Wallis Simpson, and he wanted to marry her. But kings weren't allowed to marry divorced women. So Edward had to choose between being King and marrying the woman he loved. He chose to marry Wallis, and abdicated (gave up the throne).

Edward VIII
20 January – 11 December 1936

George VI was shy, had a stutter, and didn't really want to be King. But when his brother Edward abdicated, George had no choice. The day before Edward gave up the throne, George visited his mother. He wrote in his diary, "when I told her what had happened, I broke down and sobbed like a child."

This photograph shows George at work in Buckingham Palace with his elder daughter, Princess Elizabeth. He wanted her to be better prepared to rule the country than he had been.

George was crowned with the St. Edward's Crown, a copy of Edward the Confessor's crown. It's made from solid gold, and is very heavy. It was made for Charles II, after the original was destroyed by Cromwell, and it's been used to crown almost every monarch since.

This is the Imperial State Crown. It's usually used at the end of the coronation service. It contains pearls owned by Elizabeth I, almost 3,000 diamonds, and sapphires which survived from Edward the Confessor's crown.

George and his wife Elizabeth stayed in London during the Second World War, even though the city was being bombed, and they visited people who had lost their homes. George's loyalty to his people made him very popular.

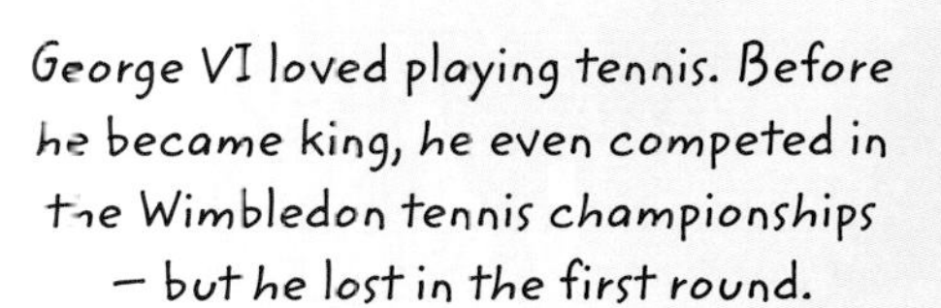

During the war, George's elder daughter, Elizabeth, trained as a driver and mechanic and drove an ambulance. This picture shows her changing a wheel.

George VI loved playing tennis. Before he became king, he even competed in the Wimbledon tennis championships – but he lost in the first round.

This photo shows George with his family and Prime Minister Winston Churchill celebrating the end of the Second World War in 1945.

Left – right:
Princess Elizabeth, Queen Elizabeth, Winston Churchill, George VI, Princess Margaret.

In 1952, George died, aged 56. His wife Elizabeth became known as the Queen Mother when her daughter Elizabeth became Queen. She was extremely popular with the British people and died in 2002, aged 101.

The royal family today

Queen Elizabeth II has reigned for well over 50 years. During this time, the role of the monarchy has changed dramatically, and media interest in the royal family has grown and grown.

Elizabeth II's coronation took place on June 2, 1953. It was the first coronation to be shown on television. TV was a relatively new invention, and many families bought their first ever TV set especially to watch it.

This picture shows Elizabeth with her husband, Prince Philip, on her coronation day. They met just before the Second World War, and married in 1947.

They have four children: Charles, Anne, Andrew and Edward, and eight grandchildren.

Prince Charles, the Queen's eldest son, is the heir to the throne. He was crowned Prince of Wales by the Queen when he was 20 years old.

Prince Charles with the Queen at the investiture (crowning ceremony) at Caernarfon Castle in Wales in 1969

In 1981, Prince Charles married Lady Diana Spencer. Millions of people watched their wedding on television. The couple had two children, but they separated in 1992.

Diana became one of the most photographed women in the world. In 1997, she died in a car crash in Paris. Over a million people lined the streets to watch her funeral procession.

Prince Charles does lots of charity work. The 'Prince's Charities' is the largest group of charities in Britain. Charles is particularly interested in helping young people and saving the environment.

Charles even has his own range of organic food products.

Anne, the Princess Royal, takes part in more than 500 public engagements a year. She's also Colonel-in-Chief of several military regiments in Britain and the Commonwealth.

Anne is also famous for her horse riding skills, and she has competed in the Olympic Games.

Prince Charles is photographed here on holiday in Switzerland with his two sons, William (right) and Harry (left).
Prince Harry is now an officer in the army.

In 2005, Prince Charles married Camilla Parker-Bowles.

Prince William studied at St. Andrews University in Scotland, then joined the RAF, where he trained to fly planes and helicopters. In 2011, he married Catherine Middleton, who he had met at university.

Like their father, William and Harry have set up their own charitable foundation. They do all sorts of things to help raise money for young people and the environment. In 2008, they went on an eight-day sponsored motorcycle ride around Africa.

Elizabeth II

In the early hours of April 21, 1926, King George V and his wife, Queen Mary, heard the news that their first grandchild had been born. As the daughter of the King's second son, no one at the time imagined that the little princess would one day be Queen.

A month later, the baby was christened at Buckingham Palace. She was named Elizabeth Alexandra Mary, after her mother, grandmother and great-grandmother.

On her sixth birthday, Elizabeth (and her little sister Margaret Rose) were given a little straw thatched cottage by the people of Wales.

Elizabeth and family at the 'Welsh House'

Elizabeth was only 10 when her father was crowned King George VI – after her grandfather died and her uncle Edward VIII abdicated. She's standing between the King and Queen in this coronation photograph.

Now she was heir to the throne, her life was about to change forever.

Elizabeth's father gave her corgis (a breed of dog) as a present when she was a child. She's had them as pets ever since.

In November 1947, soon after her 21st birthday, Elizabeth married Prince Philip of Greece, a naval officer, at Westminster Abbey. The new couple became known as the Duke and Duchess of Edinburgh.

In 1952, Elizabeth and Philip set off on an official tour of Australia and New Zealand. They stopped off in Kenya, where they received the sad news that the King was dead. Elizabeth flew back immediately to take up her role as Queen.

Queen Elizabeth's Coronation in 1953

The Queen spends some of her summer at Balmoral in Scotland. Here she is with Prince Philip and their three eldest children: Charles, Anne and Andrew.

The Queen has now reigned for so long, she is the longest serving head of state in the world. She has worked with 12 different British prime ministers.

This photograph was taken in her study. Notice her pet corgi dogs under her desk.

As head of the Commonwealth, the group of nations made up of former colonies, the Queen often travels abroad meeting other world leaders.

One of the Queen's official titles is Commander in Chief of the British Armed Forces. Here she is at a ceremony called Trooping the Colour.

Jubilees to mark her time as Queen have been celebrated with processions, fireworks and street parties.

The Silver Jubilee (25 years) in 1977 was followed by the Golden Jubilee (50 years) in 2003. In 2012, the Queen celebrates her Diamond Jubilee: 60 years on the throne.

You can find out more by going to the Usborne Quicklinks Website at www.usborne-quicklinks.com and typing in the keywords "kings and queens sticker book".

Acknowledgements

Digital manipulation by Nick Wakeford
Picture research by Ruth King and Sam Noonan

Cover: Queen Victoria © Hulton Archive/Getty Images; Henry VIII © Walker Art Gallery, National Museums Liverpool/The Bridgeman Art Library; Elizabeth I © Woburn Abbey, Bedfordshire, UK/The Bridgeman Art Library; Elizabeth II © Victoria and Albert Museum, London; **02-03 Early English kings:** Edward the Confessor © National Archive/HIP/TopFoto; William the Conqueror, with special authorisation of the city of Bayeux Giraudon/The Bridgeman Art Library; William II © The British Library/HIP/TopFoto; Henry I © Chetham's Library, Manchester, UK/The Bridgeman Art Library; King Stephen © The British Library Board. All Rights Reserved/Bridgeman Art Library; Matilda © The British Library Board. All Rights Reserved/Bridgeman Art Library; **04-05 Early Scottish kings:** Macbeth © Hulton Archive/Getty Images; Malcolm III © National Library of Scotland. Licensor www.scran.ac.uk; David I © Private Collection/The Bridgeman Art Library; Alexander III © The Masters and Fellows of Corpus Christi College, Cambridge; John Balliol © National Library of Scotland, Edinburgh, Scotland/The Bridgeman Art Library; Robert I © National Library of Scotland, Edinburgh, Scotland/The Bridgeman Art Library; **06-07 The Plantagenets:** Henry II © British Library/HIP/TopFoto; Richard I © The Granger Collection/TopFoto; King John © The British Library Board. All Rights Reserved/The Bridgeman Art Library; Edward I © The British Library Board. All Rights Reserved/The Bridgeman Art Library; Edward II © TopFoto/HIP; Edward III © Private Collection/The Bridgeman Art Library; Richard II © Westminster Abbey, London, UK/The Bridgeman Art Library; **08-09 War of the Roses:** Henry IV © Philip Mould Ltd, London/The Bridgeman Art Library; Henry V © National Portrait Gallery, London, UK/The Bridgeman Art Library; Henry VI © Private Collection/The Bridgeman Art Library; Edward IV © Musee Thomas Dobree-Musee Archeologique, Nantes, France/Giraudon/The Bridgeman Art Library; Edward V © Lambeth Palace Library, London, UK/The Bridgeman Art Library; Richard III © Private Collection/The Bridgeman Art Library; **10-11 The Tudors:** Henry VII © Society of Antiquaries of London, UK/The Bridgeman Art Library; Henry VIII © Walker Art Gallery, National Museums, Liverpool/The Bridgeman Art Library; Catherine of Aragon © Private Collection/Philip Mould Ltd, London/The Bridgeman Art Library; Anne Boleyn © Hever Castle, Kent, UK/The Bridgeman Art Library; Jane Seymour © Kunsthistorisches Museum, Vienna, Austria/The Bridgeman Art Library; Anne of Cleves © Louvre, Paris, France/Giraudon/The Bridgeman Art Library; Catherine Howard © Private Collection/Philip Mould Ltd, London/The Bridgeman Art Library; Catherine Parr © National Portrait Gallery, London, UK/The Bridgeman Art Library; **12-13 More Tudors:** Edward VI © Private Collection/Philip Mould Ltd, London, UK/The Bridgeman Art Library; The Execution of Lady Jane Grey © National Gallery, London, UK/The Bridgeman Art Library; Mary I © Society of Antiquaries of London, UK/The Bridgeman Art Library; Elizabeth I © National Portrait Gallery, London, UK/The Bridgeman Art Library; Elizabeth I Armada Portrait © Woburn Abbey, Bedfordshire, UK/The Bridgeman Art Library; Sir Walter Raleigh © Kunsthistorisches Museum, Vienna, Austria/The Bridgeman Art Library; **14-15 Scottish Stewarts:** James I © Scottish National Portrait Gallery, Edinburgh, Scotland/The Bridgeman Art Library; Robert III © National Library of Scotland; James II © Wuerttembergische Landesbibliothek, Stuttgart, Cod. hist. 4° 141, p. 97; James III © Scottish National Portrait Gallery, Edinburgh, Scotland/The Bridgeman Art Library; James IV © Scottish National Portrait Gallery, Edinburgh, Scotland/The Bridgeman Art Library; Scottish Crown © National Library of Scotland. Licensor www.scran.ac.uk; James V © Private Collection/ Philip Mould Ltd, London/The Bridgeman Art Library; Mary Queen of Scots © Victoria & Albert Museum, London, UK/The Bridgeman Art Library; **16-17 The Stuarts:** James I © Prado, Madrid, Spain/The Bridgeman Art Library; Guy Fawkes and conspirators © Lambeth Palace Library, London, UK/ The Bridgeman Art Library; Charles I © His Grace The Duke of Norfolk, Arundel Castle/The Bridgeman Art Library; Henrietta Maria © His Grace The Duke of Norfolk, Arundel Castle/The Bridgeman Art Library; Oliver Cromwell © Private Collection/The Bridgeman Art Library; Prince Rupert of the Rhine © Petworth House, West Sussex, UK/National Trust Photographic Library/Derrick E. Witty/The Bridgeman Art Library; **18-19 Restoring the Stuarts:** Charles II © Private Collection/The Bridgeman Art Library; Samuel Pepys © National Portrait Gallery, London, UK/The Bridgeman Art Library; James II © National Portrait Gallery, London, UK/The Bridgeman Art Library; William and Mary © James Brittain/The Bridgeman Art Library; Queen Anne © Private Collection/Philip Mould Ltd, London/The Bridgeman Art Library; **20-21 The Hanoverians:** George I © The Crown Estate/The Bridgeman Art Library; Robert Walpole © British Museum, London, UK/The Bridgeman Art Library; James Stuart © Private Collection/ Philip Mould Ltd, London/The Bridgeman Art Library; George II © The Trustees of Goodwood Collection/The Bridgeman Art Library; Charles Stuart © The Drambuie Collection, Edinburgh, Scotland/The Bridgeman Art Library; **22-23 More Hanoverians:** George III © Private Collection/Peter Newark American Pictures/The Bridgeman Art Library; Queen Charlotte © National Gallery, London, UK/The Bridgeman Art Library; George IV © Roy Miles Fine Paintings/The Bridgeman Art Library; George IV cartoon © City of London/HIP/Topfoto; Queen Caroline © Guildhall Art Gallery, City of London/ The Bridgeman Art Library; William IV © English Heritage. NMR/The Bridgeman Art Library; **24-25 Victoria and the house of Saxe-Coburg-Gotha:** Queen Victoria © Hulton Archive/Stringer/Getty Images; Victoria and Albert © Hulton Archive/ Stringer/Getty Images; Victoria and family around the Christmas tree © Hulton Archive/ Stringer/Getty Images; Crystal Palace © Mary Evans Picture Library; Queen Victoria and Princess Helena © Hulton-Deutsch Collection/CORBIS; Edward VII © Private Collection/Ken Welsh/The Bridgeman Art Library; **26-27 The Windsors:** George V © Hulton Archive/ Stringer/Getty Images; Edward VIII © Popperfoto/Getty Images; George VI and Princess Elizabeth © Lisa Sheridan/Studio Lisa/Getty Images; St. Edward's Crown and Imperial State Crown © Tom Hanley/Alamy; Princess Elizabeth as a mechanic © Roger Viollet/Getty Images; Royal Family on balcony © Reg Speller/Stringer/Getty Images; Queen Mother © Jayne Fincher.Photo Int/Alamy; **28-29 The Royal Family Today:** Elizabeth II and Philip © AFP/Getty Images; Prince Charles and Diana wedding © Trinity Mirror/Mirrorpix/Alamy; Prince Charles investiture © Keystone Pictures USA/ Alamy; Princess Anne © Rex Features; Princes Charles, William and Harry in Klosters © Trinity Mirror/Mirrorpix/Alamy; Prince Charles and Camilla wedding © Anwar Hussein Collection/ROTA/WireImage/Getty Images; Prince William and Catherine wedding © Tim Rooke/Rex Features; **30-31 Elizabeth II:** Christening Elizabeth II © Hulton Archive/Getty Images; Coronation George VI © Getty Images; Royal Family, Welsh house © Hulton Archive/Getty Images; Elizabeth II wedding © Hulton-Deutsch Collection/CORBIS; Family at Balmoral © Press Association Images; Elizabeth II at desk © Hulton Archive/Getty Images; Elizabeth II trooping the colour © Press Association Images; Elizabeth II © Anwar Hussein/Getty Images.

This edition published in 2012 by Usborne Publishing Ltd, 83-85 Saffron Hill, London EC1N 8RT, England.

Early English kings pages 2-3

Early Scottish kings pages 4-5

The Plantagenets pages 6-7

Early Scottish kings pages 4-5

The Wars of the Roses pages 8-9

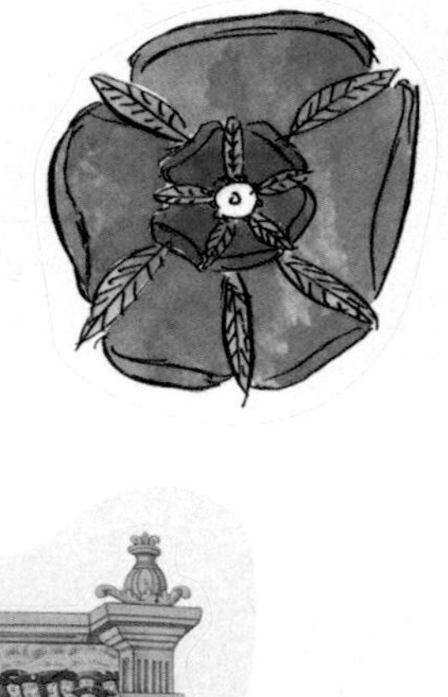

The Tudors pages 10-11

More Tudors pages 12-13

The Tudors pages 10-11

The Scottish Stewarts pages 14-15

The Stuarts pages 16-17

Restoring the Stuarts pages 18-19

The Stuarts pages 16-17

The Hanoverians pages 20-21

More Hanoverians pages 22-23

Queen Victoria pages 24-25

More Hanoverians pages 22-23

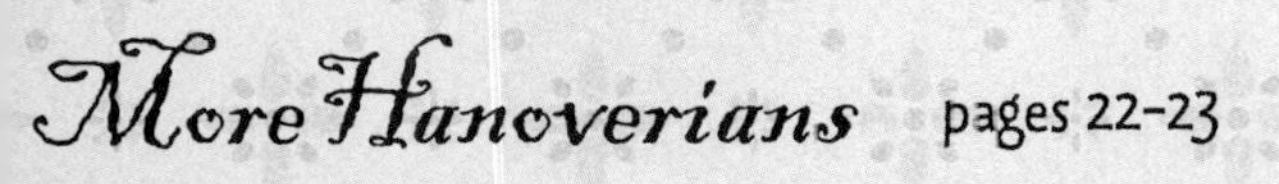

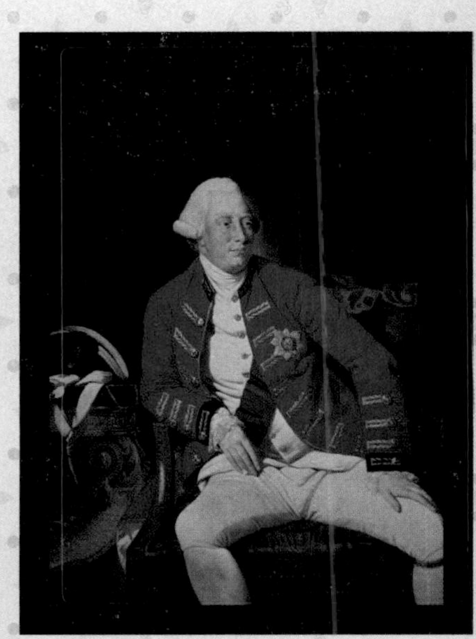

The Windsors pages 26-27

The royal family today pages 28-29

Elizabeth II pages 30-31

The royal family today pages 28-29